United States
Department of
Agriculture

Forest Service

Forest
Products
Laboratory

State and
Private Forestry

Technology
Marketing Unit

General
Technical
Report
FPL–GTR–175

Small-Diameter Success Stories III

Jean Livingston

Abstract

More than 73 million acres of our national forests and millions more in public and private forestlands are in need of some form of restoration. Our forests are declining in health because of major changes over the years in forest structure and composition. However, restoration of these overstocked stands is extremely expensive. If new, economical, and value-added uses for thinned material can be found, forest restoration costs could be offset as the threat of catastrophic wildfires is reduced. This is the third document that tells the story of several wood product businesses and communities across the country that are successfully using thinning material from forest restoration projects and converting it into wood products and biomass energy. Telling these small-diameter success stories is intended to accomplish several goals but three in particular: (1) clarify and enumerate the value and importance of funding programs to help small businesses and forestry-dependent communities; (2) provide marketing tools for these businesses; and (3) create a forest restoration networking system across the United States.

Keywords: small-diameter timber, forest restoration, roundwood, small business, unmerchantable timber, Woody Biomass Utilization grant, Bureau of Land Management, stewardship contracting

Acknowledgments

It takes the help of so many to put together a document like this. I sincerely thank the individuals, businesses, and communities who provided me with personal interviews and tours of their organizations. It is always a pleasure and, in some cases, it has been a little exhilarating for me when gathering these interviews. Special thanks to Terry Fairbanks who went the extra mile to help provide material for the Bureau of Land Management section. Also, thanks to JoAnn Benisch, who designed the cover of this document; to James Anderson, for editing; and to Tivoli Gough, for design and layout. Most importantly, thanks to Susan LeVan-Green, without whose support and foresight this document would never have been written.

April 2008

Livingston, Jean. 2008. Small-diameter success stories III. Gen. Tech. Rep. FPL-GTR-175. Madison, WI: U.S. Department of Agriculture, Forest Service, Forest Products Laboratory. 31 p.

A limited number of free copies of this publication are available to the public from the Forest Products Laboratory, One Gifford Pinchot Drive, Madison, WI 53726–2398. This publication is also available online at www.fpl.fs.fed.us. Laboratory publications are sent to hundreds of libraries in the United States and elsewhere.

The Forest Products Laboratory is maintained in cooperation with the University of Wisconsin.

Conversion Table

To convert from inch–pound unit	To metric unit	Multiply by
inch (in.)	millimeter (mm)	25.4
foot (ft)	meter (m)	0.3048
mile	kilometer (km)	1.609
pound (lb)	kilogram (kg)	0.4536
ton	tonne (t)	0.9071
acre	hectare (ha)	0.4047
square foot (ft^2)	square meter (m^2)	9.290×10^{-2}
board foot	cubic meter (m^3)	2.360×10^{-3}
cubic yard (yd^3)	cubic meter (m^3)	0.7646
pound per square inch (lb/in^2)	pascal (Pa)	6.895×10^3
pound per square foot (lb/ft^2)	pascal (Pa)	47.88

Contents

Small-Diameter Success Stories III

Jean Livingston
Communications Specialist (retired)
U.S. Forest Service
State & Private Forestry, Technology Marketing Unit
Forest Products Laboratory
Madison, Wisconsin

Foreword

This is the third edition of *Small-Diameter Success Stories*, by Jean Livingston. Each edition has focused on stories of the energetic and indomitable spirit of the many entrepreneurs who are using the woody biomass material that is being removed from our forestlands to reduce (1) the threat of wildfires, (2) the impact of insects and disease, and (3) the impact of catastrophic weather events such as hurricanes and wind storms. These include people like Jim and Lynn Jungwirth from Hayfork, California (first edition), who turn small-diameter Douglas fir into flooring; Phil Archuletta from Mountainaire, New Mexico (second edition), who uses juniper in his wood–plastic composite signs; and Link and Jennifer Phillippi from Cave Junction, Oregon (this third edition), who burn forest slash piles in their 1.5 MW wood boiler. These enterprises have taken woody biomass material that traditionally had little value and highlighted how "junk" or low-value wood can be made into studs, poles, pallets, pellets, flooring, molding and millwork, or biomass energy. Each edition has demonstrated projects throughout the nation. We hope that the examples highlighted in this three-volume series have helped create or expand new opportunities for both forest managers and rural communities. More importantly, we hope that you have a better understanding of the people behind these projects and are inspired by their commitment and dedication.

However, this is the last of the series. Our national interest for using woody biomass has increased due to $100/barrel oil. The U.S. Department of Energy, the U.S. Department of Interior, and the U.S. Department of Agriculture have initiatives aimed at stimulating the use of all biomass for both biofuels and biopower. The Energy Independence and Security Act of 2007 includes the use of woody biomass in the portfolio of feedstocks for renewable energy. The momentum for renewable energy from biomass is building and changes will be happening very fast and reported in comprehensive compendiums. Now the focus for the Forest Service will be to ensure that woody biomass removals are conducted in a sustainable manner, which improves the Nation's forest health and provides local economic opportunity.

However, another critical reason for discontinuing this series is that our writer–editor Jean Livingston has retired from the Forest Service after 37 years of dedicated service. Therefore, this issue is dedicated to Jean and her untiring efforts to capture in print the spirit of the businesses, organizations, and communities dedicated to helping improve our forestlands. We wish Jean the best in her retirement—but retirement is probably not the best description for her new endeavors. Jean will continue to work for many rural communities, helping them explain their stories, problems, and successes.

During Jean's many travels to capture these stories, she has encountered many obstacles, such as bad weather, plane delays, detours, dangerous fugitives, road blocks, and the most worrisome of delays—having to drive in unknown regions during snowstorms and blizzards. Her stories on her return to our unit always captured our imagination as we envisioned her hanging off a cliff in an eternity of blinding snow. If you see her, please ask her about her travels preparing these stories—you will be thrilled and entertained.

Personally, I want to thank Jean for always tackling these assignments with renewed dedication and enthusiasm for meeting and capturing the essence of the folks contained in these pages. Through her stories, one gains a greater appreciation for the folks out on the ground. Jean never said no, although she may later have wished that she did. However, I suspect her fear of a *Small-Diameter Success Stories IV* may have been the reason for her retirement. Jean, best wishes in your next endeavor.

Susan LeVan-Green
Program Manager
U.S. Forest Service
State & Private Forestry, Technology Marketing Unit
Forest Products Laboratory
Madison, Wisconsin

Introduction

More than 73 million acres of our national forests and millions more in public and private forestlands are in need of some form of restoration. Forests are declining in health because of major changes over the years in forest structure and composition. This trend has a negative impact on the growth of native trees and plants, wildlife habitat, and watersheds. Unhealthy forests present a high risk for catastrophic fires and epidemic insect infestation and disease.

Restoration of these overstocked stands, through mechanical thinning or prescribed burning, will remove most of the small-diameter and woody biomass material, thus helping the forest to recover its natural structure and ecological functions. Mechanical thinning is usually completed prior to prescribed burning. However, mechanical forest thinning is extremely expensive. If new, economical, and value-added uses for thinned material can be found, forest restoration costs could be offset as the threat of catastrophic wildfires is reduced.

To help accomplish forest restoration, various approaches are being taken to complete the necessary work and simultaneously contribute to the economic growth of communities. Restoration of our forests will persist as long as we continue working together for the ecological health of our forests and the economic health of forestry-based rural communities.

This is the third document that tells the story of several wood product businesses and communities across the country that are successfully using thinning material from forest restoration projects and converting it into wood products and biomass energy. Telling these small-diameter stories is intended to accomplish several goals but three in particular: (1) clarify and enumerate the value and importance of funding programs to help small businesses

All Americans have an obligation to protect the Earth and a responsibility to be good stewards of our land, and my Administration has made forest health a high priority. Under the Healthy Forest Initiative, we are helping to protect the American people, their communities, and the environment from potentially devastating wildfires. Together we can conserve our woodlands and help leave a lasting legacy for future generations.

*- President George W. Bush,
National Forest Products Week,
October 2007*

National Woody Biomass Utilization Grant Program

The National Woody Biomass Utilization Grant Program (administered by the State & Private Forestry Technology Marketing Unit, located at the Forest Products Laboratory in Madison, Wisconsin) is intended to help improve forest restoration activities by using and creating markets for small-diameter material and low-valued trees removed from hazardous fuel reduction activities. These funds are targeted to help communities, entrepreneurs, and others (such as state, local, and Tribal governments; school districts; non-profit organizations; businesses; companies; corporations; public utility districts; fire districts; conservation districts; ports) turn residues from hazardous fuel reduction projects into marketable forest products and/or energy products.

This grant program has three principal goals:

- Help reduce management costs by increasing value of biomass and other forest products generated by hazardous fuel treatments

- Create incentives and/or reduce business risk for increased use of biomass from or near national forestlands (must include National Forest System lands, however, may also include other lands such as Bureau of Land Management, Tribal, state, local, and private)

- Institute projects that target and help remove economic and market barriers to using small-diameter trees and woody biomass

and forestry-dependent communities; (2) provide marketing tools for these businesses; and (3) create a networking system for similar businesses across the United States.

Some of the following stories describe how the Forest Service's National Woody Biomass Utilization Grant Program (see sidebar) is working to improve forest restoration by helping to create markets from this thinned material. Some stories explain how communities and small businesses are working together to solve our nation's forest crisis. The final section discusses the Bureau of Land Management (BLM) and how they work closely with the U.S. Forest Service. In addition, two completed BLM stewardship contracts are described. Observations from those stewardship contractors and comments from the contractor who helped establish the baseline for stewardship contracting in Ashland, Oregon, are given.

Bearlodge Forest Products, Inc.

Incorporated in 1977, Bearlodge Forest Products, Inc., is a three-generation family business. Located in northeast Wyoming, near the town of Hulett, it is surrounded by the beautiful Black Hills National Forest.

The Black Hills National Forest is located in western South Dakota and northeastern Wyoming, covering 1.2 million acres; 160,000 of these are in Wyoming. From a distance, these pine-covered hills, rising several thousand feet above the surrounding prairie, appear black, thus the name Black Hills.

Family interest in the sawmill/logging business goes back to Great-Grandfather A.C. Neiman and his sons. Eventually, A.C. Neiman's son, Henry, and his three sons (Dan, Phil, and Walt) incorporated the business known today as Bearlodge Forest Products, Inc. In 2001, Henry Neiman's son, Dan, and his wife, Ann, purchased the business, and in 2002, Dan Neiman's daughter, Dena, and son-in-law, Doug Mills, joined the company.

Everyone in the family is part of the business and each has their specialty area. The business office is located alongside the mill and doubles as Dena and Doug's ranch-style home; they live in the lower level. At Bearlodge Forest Products, family comes first and practicing responsible land stewardship comes naturally.

Bearlodge Forest Products produces more than 6 million board feet of material each year from ponderosa pine. They specialize in products such as wood pallets, wood pellets, custom sawn lumber and timbers, and CHINK-A-LOG® siding.

CHINK-A-LOG® is unique to Bearlodge Forest Products—a product that necessitates explanation. It is an alternative to conventional log cabin siding and presents a natural, authentic log cabin look.

"We offer two profiles of CHINK-A-LOG® siding," says Dena. "Both are 7-1/4 inches wide and available in random lengths, but one is flat and is 3/4 inch thick, and the other has a radius and is 1-1/2 inches thick."

Dena and Doug Mills

Newly designed company sign

CHINK-A-LOG® siding comes as a package. There are custom window bucks, as well as turned log corners. Bearlodge Forest Products offers the Perma-Chink System® products (to stain, finish, and chink your project) and all the tools needed (the same tools needed to install any other type of wood siding). Bearlodge also offers a how-to-install video.

According to U.S. Forest Service District Ranger Steven Kozel, "In recent years this area [Black Hills National Forest] has experienced severe drought, compounded with wildfires of historic proportions for size and intensity, and has made treatment of high-density, fire-adapted stands that are at high risk for significant stand-replacement fire a priority."

Kozel also says that they will continue to have fuel reduction projects on about 500 acres per year on the Black Hills National Forest in sizes that could be utilized for pallet production. "Without a market outlet for this material, taxpayers will pay higher costs per acre for masticating, chipping, mulching, or otherwise shredding the woody biomass and leaving it spread over the forest floor." Kozel says that a facility like Bearlodge Forest Products is a perfect outlet for this material.

Each year, Bearlodge Forest Products utilizes 1.5 million board feet of products other than logs (POLs) for pallet parts. This wood is then manufactured into pallet parts for approximately 100,000 pallets per year.

Family owner, Dena Mills, says that they sometimes have difficulty purchasing lumber that is of adequate quality to use for making pallets. To meet their market demand and to ensure quality, Bearlodge Forest Products was determined to install a pallet cant processing system to produce pallet boards and stringers (pallet parts).

To help finance the pallet cant processing system,

Bearlodge Forest Products, Inc.
1506 Hwy. 24, P.O. Box 248
Hulett, WY 82720

Dan Neiman (Dena's father)

CHINK-A-LOG® siding

in 2007 they applied for and received a Woody Biomass Utilization grant, a program sponsored by the U.S. Forest Service. Their Pendu cant processing system was installed at Bearlodge Forest Products in the winter of 2007–2008.

"With this system we can now utilize 133,000 board feet of POLs generated from the Forest Service's hazardous fuel treatments," says Dena. "Also, we now have the ability to produce about 200,000 pallets, doubling our annual production. In addition, the sawdust produced as a result of the cant-line is converted into wood pellets, another one of our value-added products."

The owners of Bearlodge Forest Products are well known for promoting responsible forestry and have been in the small-wood utilization business for 30 years. The wood resource needed to sustain this business will undoubtedly be there for generations to come. In addition, I feel confident that this company will continue to maintain their strong stewardship values, which will be passed on to future family generations of Bearlodge Forest Products.

Pallets made by Bearlodge

Big Sky Forest Products

As result of the 2006 National Woody Biomass Grant program, Big Sky Forest Products was able to purchase a small-log chipper, which is the final piece of equipment needed for their plan to efficiently turn low-value logs into the highest value possible. Big Sky Forest Products, located near St. Regis, Montana, was purchased in 1996 and is a profitable and efficiently run small roundwood facility.

In 2000, St. Regis was listed as having a population of 315 people. The town is surrounded by mountains with thousands of miles of creeks and rivers and numerous lakes, forests, hiking trails, ski slopes, snowmobile runs, wildlife, fishing, and whitewater rafting. The town was once a shipping point for the lumber industry, which is now minimal. Currently, the community is primarily a tourist area.

Gary Suppiger operates three roundwood manufacturing plants: Big Sky in St. Regis and Panhandle Forest Products in Priest River, Idaho, and in Cranbrook, British Columbia, Canada. In 1966, Panhandle merged with Big Sky, which was originally owned and operated by brothers Harley and Steve Freeman. Steve manages production at the mill in St. Regis.

When I visited Big Sky, Suppiger explained how the newly purchased small-log chipper "was a culmination of a series of projects designed to efficiently process small-diameter, low-value, and previously not merchantable logs into marketable products."

Steve Freeman designed and fabricated all the roundwood manufacturing machinery at Big Sky. He said, "Through National Fire Plan funds, Big Sky was able to complete the first phase of our small-log merchandizing expansion in 2003 with a new log deck, including a chop saw, log transfer, and electronic sorting system. The second phase included the small-log debarker that was installed in 2005."

Suppiger said that they process unmerchantable logs into doweled and peeled roundwood products such as fencing, poles, horse jump rails, doweled furniture grade rounds, half-round fence rails, and lattias. Their highest valued product is their dowelled logs. Byproducts include wood chips for pulp, clean fines for particleboard, and bark for hog fuel or landscape mulch.

"No fiber is wasted. The entire log is utilized to manufacture a marketable product. We utilize virtually every log without respect for species, straightness, soundness, size, or dryness," stated Suppiger.

Big Sky employs six people for an 8-hour work shift. With the purchase of the small-log chipper, they plan to add two more employees to their payroll.

Eighty percent of Big Sky's supply is from public forest-lands such as the Idaho Panhandle, Kootenai, and Flathead

Big Sky Forest Products, Regis, Montana

Gary Suppiger

Operation at Big Sky

National Forests, the Flathead Indian Reservation, and Montana Department of Natural Resources.

All products are marketed through their parent company, Panhandle Forest Products, which has a sales force of one full-time and one part-time person. Their sales strategy is to sell user direct and offer customer delivery.

> Big Sky Forest Products
> P.O. Box 489
> St. Regis, MT 59866

Debarking roundwood

Kevin Chamberlain, Director of the County Office of Economic Development, and B.J. McComb, County Commissioner, strongly support Big Sky Forest Products. Chamberlain says that "Big Sky has been a partner with the county for many years. The fact that their business is thriving is testimony to their hard wood and dedication. Any business tied to roundwood or small-diameter timber is difficult, but through their attention to efficiencies and sound marketing, they are making it work."

Chadron State College

The community of Chadron, Nebraska, was moving toward using their abundance of woody biomass as the source of energy for a forest biomass steam plant at Chadron State College long before many of us even thought about this possibility.

The town of Chadron is a community of about 6,000 and is located in northwest Nebraska near the scenic Pine Ridge. In addition to some of the best cattle ranching land, this area boasts of its recreational opportunities such as fishing, hunting, and cross-country skiing.

Located within the town of Chadron, Chadron State College is the only 4-year graduate-degree granting college in western Nebraska. The 281-acre campus has almost 3,000 students, 24 buildings, and 1.1 million square feet of floor space. As one of the larger employers in the region, the college employs 300 people.

The community and Chadron State College also boast about the forest biomass steam plant that was installed at the college about 18 years ago. H. Doak Nickerson, Northwest District Forester for the Nebraska Forest Service, tells the story of how it all began.

"We initially got the idea from Northwest Missouri State University in Maryville, Missouri. We were aware of their wood-burning system and knew they were saving money. A delegation of community leaders from Chadron State College, Nebraska Forest Service, and the Nebraska National Forest came together and decided to take a road trip to Missouri to see their facility in operation."

Their trip to Missouri left a lasting impression on the Nebraska delegation. After returning home, the Nebraska Forest Service worked with Chadron State College staff to first develop a resource analysis and then an engineering feasibility study for possible installation.

"We knew we had the volume of wood resource that was necessary and the analysis from the college gave us positive feedback. However, at that time, the college did not have the capital investment fund available to follow through with the plan," said Nickerson.

So the forest biomass plan sat on the shelf for at least 5 years. In 1989, this community experienced one of the worst forest fires in the state's history, where 25,000 acres of the Fort Robinson Wilderness Area were destroyed in less than a week.

Nickerson said, "Just 1 month after the U.S. Forest Service had designated part of this land as the Soldier Creek Wilderness Area—catastrophic wildfires burned it to the ground!"

In a local meeting following these devastating fires, land owners, agencies, and others in the community came

H. Doak Nickerson, Northwest District Forester, Nebraska Forest Service

Forest biomass steam plant

together to see how they could turn this devastating fire into some positive action. The fact was that a tremendous volume of wood would go to waste if they didn't do something. Eventually the resource analysis and engineering study for a forest biomass plant that had been sitting on the shelf for years came into play. In the end, State Senator Sandy Scofield came to the community's rescue by putting together an innovative, renewable energy package for the College.

Nickerson said "It's too bad it took a disaster to get the project moving, nevertheless, we received state appropriated funds to purchase and install the wood-burning system within a year."

According to Nickerson, two wood energy boiler units (6,000 and 12,000 lb/h) went into operation in 1991 at a cost of $1 million. Wood fuel storage capacity is 100 tons, with maximum daily consumption at 50 tons. Annual demand

Chadron State College
Chadron, NE 69337-2433

Trucks delivering woody supply to biomass steam plant

is between 7,000 and 8,000 tons, with wood ash generation an efficient 2% to 3%. Energy savings are averaging more than $130,000 per year compared with natural gas, resulting in a capital investment payback in 7 years! Because of these results, the college added a $1,350,000 air-conditioning chiller in 2004.

The majority of the college's wood fuel comes from logging slash piles and fuel treatment thinning in the wildland–urban interface on privately owned lands. Only a small percentage of supply is from state lands, and an even smaller percentage is from federal lands. In northwest Nebraska, two-thirds of forests are privately owned.

The supplier for Chadron State College is an in-woods chipping contractor who is part of a struggling forest products industry that infuses between $5 to $10 million per year into the local economy.

"I think if the College had it to do over again, they would have done a couple things differently," Nickerson said. "Instead of stockpiling the chips outdoors on the bare ground, they may have invested additional funds in an enclosed chip storage area. If the chips had been stored in a concrete lined bunker under roof, they may have avoided losing our entire chip inventory to the 2006 fires that nearly burned the college and town to the ground."

Nickerson noted that the college's success in pursuing fossil fuel independence is catching on in Chadron. The community is now in the early stages of constructing a new, state-of-the art hospital. As part of the engineering design for this facility, it is being built to allow for a ready "plug-in" of an adjoining wood energy plant sometime in the future. This conversion would make wood the primary energy source, with natural gas taking a back-up role and diesel fuel serving in emergencies only.

This community is fortunate that their leaders had the vision and foresight 20 years ago to convert Chadron State College to a forest biomass steam facility. I am sure that active stewardship and management of the Pine Ridge forestlands of northwest Nebraska will continue to sustain a continuous flow of forest biomass for both Chadron State College and the community's new hospital.

England Sawmills

In the fall of 2006, England Sawmills, located near Salmon, Idaho, improved its capacity, decreased its shipping costs, increased its price per board foot, and gained the option of offering two new high-valued products. These achievements were a direct result of a newly installed dry kiln, partially funded from U.S. Forest Service National Woody Biomass Utilization grant dollars.

Salmon is located on the Salmon River in central Idaho, near the Montana border, and close to the Salmon–Challis National Forest. The legendary Lewis and Clark Expedition passed through Salmon in 1805, and it is the birthplace of Sacajawea's people, the AgaiDika Shoshone. The area is well known for its superior white-water rafting, hunting, and fishing. This small community of about 3,000 has been hit hard the past 10 years because of job losses in the mining and timber industries. The Federal government and the agricultural industry are the only major employers in the area.

Since 1999, Gary England has owned and operated England Sawmills, and it is the only small-diameter sawmill located within 150 miles of the Salmon–Challis National Forest, from which the sawmill gets almost all its supply. Gary is a very proud American who recently installed a large American flag on top of his wood chipper. The flag took priority over putting up a sign that identified the name of his sawmill.

The Salmon–Challis National Forest covers more than 4.3 million acres of east-central Idaho. Included within its boundaries are 1.3 million acres of the largest wilderness area in the continental United States.

"We have a dangerous fuel buildup condition on the Salmon–Challis National Forest that is contributing to poor forest health, potential for catastrophic wildfires, and a threat to communities from wildfires," said Bill Wood, Forest Supervisor for the U.S. Forest Service. "We are working to plan and implement fuel reduction treatments on thousands of acres in the next few years. The wood removed from these treatments will be mostly 4 to 12 inches in diameter."

Forest Supervisor Wood estimates that future projects on the Salmon–Challis National Forest will make available between 1,500 and 2,000 acres of timber annually, or 4 to 5 million board feet of timber over the next 2 years. The only local market for this timber is England Sawmills.

According to England, his mill has about $580,000 in equipment and is designed to process timber between 2 and 14 inches in diameter. It produces lumber in a variety of sizes 1 and 2 inches thick by 2 to 8 inches wide, posts and poles, and firewood. However, now that he has installed a dry kiln, England has added rough-sawn Douglas-fir flooring and house logs to his product line, which will increase his profit margin.

Overview of England's dry kiln

Gary England

Before installing the dry kiln, lumber was either air-dried, which slowed production about 3 weeks, or the lumber was shipped rough cut and green, which reduced the market value. This also increased shipping costs because he could ship only about 15,000 board feet of green material per load compared with 28,000 board feet of dried lumber.

The newly installed dry kiln increases England Sawmill's capacity from 750 thousand to about 9 million board feet per year. It has also increased his sale price per board foot because now he can sell finished lumber (instead of the rough cut lumber he sold previously). In

England Sawmills
P.O. Box 84
North Fork, ID 83466

Small-diameter supply at England Sawmills

addition, his new high-valued wood flooring and house log products will add considerably to his profit margin. In September 2006, wood flooring was selling for about $1,000 per thousand board feet.

Currently, England Sawmills has 9 employees. With the new dry kiln, England hopes to increase that to 25 employees. The dry kiln reduces drying time to 1 week and increases their production capacity to 35,000 board feet per 8-hour shift.

"Our increase in capacity and production has increased the number of employees I can hire at a living wage," said England. "The dry kiln makes it possible for me to continue production through the winter and year round, which I wasn't able to do before."

Forest Supervisor Wood says that "the addition of a dry kiln at England Sawmills should result in annual revenues for the Salmon–Challis National Forest of between $900,000 and $1,200,000 from the sale of timber and save the forest $850,000 to $1,100,000 in annual expenditures,

if we were forced to hire crews to complete these thinning treatments."

England notes that his mill runs very efficiently. All waste wood is chipped to be either used in the boiler to power his dry kiln or sold and picked up by a pulp and paper mill from Montana.

England is well known and respected by land managers in the community and the Intermountain West. Timber manufactured by England is sold to two primary buyers: Tripp Lumber and Teton West, both in Missoula, Montana.

England says "My biggest concern is supply." Now with capacity increased to about 9 million board feet per year, the raw material may not be available. According to England, not all Forest Service timber sales have been going as planned. For example, a Forest Service timber sale that was suppose to be available for bid in June 2005 did not happen until the spring of 2006. England needs a steady flow of about 2 to 4 million board feet per year to take advantage of his new production capacity. He is quick to make special note of how much he appreciates all the help and assistance he receives from both Forest Service employees and those in local government who have made it possible for him to expand his business.

Gary enjoys this line of work and has no plans to do anything else, even though at times he is frustrated with the market fluctuations and the inconsistency of supply. Gary England is a very kind, soft-spoken, patient man with a good head for business. He says his interest in the lumber business began 36 years ago working alongside his "Granddad." "This is all I ever wanted to do—I just love sitting on my porch [which overlooks his sawmill] and smelling that lumber. This wood business gets in your blood and you just can't get it out."

Forest Guild

Until a non-profit organization called Forest Guild took action, New Mexico had the highest workers' compensation insurance rates of any western state.

The Forest Guild "provides training, policy analysis, and research to foster excellence in stewardship, to support practicing foresters and allied professionals, and to engage a broader community in the challenges of forest conservation and management."

Mike DeBonis, SW Region Director for the Forest Guild, says, "One of the biggest barriers to contractors winning forest fuels reduction contracts is the excessively high workers' compensation rates in New Mexico. These rates are the highest in any of the western states. For example, in 2005 a New Mexico employer paid $79 in premiums for every $100 in payroll; other states paid an average of $25 per $100."

Workers' compensation insurance for forest thinning projects in New Mexico can be 20% to 50% of the treatment costs per acre. Many contractors employ three or fewer employees just to avoid the high cost of insurance premiums. However, a contractor with only three employees is unable to bid on large forest fuel reduction projects. In some cases, contractors do not cover their employees with workers' compensation insurance, which is not only risky for the worker, but a big risk to their business.

To help contractors with this insurance problem, in 2005 the Forest Guild sought and was awarded a $250,000 grant from the U.S. Forest Service National Woody Biomass Utilization Grant Program. The Forest Guild use of this grant included sponsoring a logger safety program with certification, which in turn would improve worker safety, reduce workers' compensation insurance losses, and help reduce the cost of removing hazardous woody biomass from national forests.

Employers in New Mexico who are "Safety Certified" qualify for an immediate reduction in insurance rates, from $79 to $30 per $100 in payroll. The Forest Guild began offering certification training around the state free of charge and sometimes even covered travel costs for attendees.

As of January 2008, the Forest Guild has offered 29 forest worker safety certification courses in locations across New Mexico; 432 workers have become safety certified. This training led the Public Regulation Commission of New Mexico to have the National Council on Compensation Insurance create a special classification for certified loggers, which means that now certified workers are eligible to receive the new rate of $30 for every $100 of payroll—a significant reduction from past rates.

"The Forest Guild's mission is to promote forestry that sustains ecosystem integrity and the well-being of human communities," said DeBonis. "The health of New

Mountainair training, May 2007 (Source: Forest Guild)

Pine Hill (Ramah Chapter of the Navajo Nation) training, June 2007 (Source: Forest Guild)

Mexico's forests is directly linked to the viability of forest-based communities and workers. By reducing the barrier of high workers' compensation insurance, the Forest Worker Safety Certification program has improved the ability of forest workers to make a living from the forests."

DeBonis notes the question from many regarding the program's sustainability: When the grant funds run

Forest Guild
P.O. Box 519
Santa Fe, NM 87504

Taos Pueblo Recertification course, June 2007 (Source: Forest Guild)

Mescalero forest crew training (Mescalero Apache Tribe), May 2007 (Source: Forest Guild)

out, will contractors and workers be willing to pay for the certification courses?

In answer to that, DeBonis says that since September 2007, three courses have been scheduled based on contractor requests. In addition to requesting the training, contractors have agreed to pay all costs associated with the course. "The fact that contractors are willing to pay the up-front cost for the training highlights the financial benefits gained through reduced workers' compensation insurance premiums," says DeBonis.

Results show that their logger safety program with certification has been a huge success. As for the future of this program—Forest Guild is working with the New Mexico Forest Industry Association (NMFIA) to serve as the program's permanent home when their National Woody Biomass Utilization grant has been exhausted. NMFIA is a newly formed association serving the forest industry, including forest workers.

Institute for Agriculture and Trade Policy

In 2005, Don Arnosti from the Institute for Agriculture and Trade Policy (IATP), along with three partners, were awarded a grant through the U.S. Forest Service National Woody Biomass Utilization Grant Program. The grant will help the Superior National Forest, its community, forestry businesses, landowners, and others ensure sustainable management of these forest lands.

IATP "promotes resilient family farms, rural communities, and ecosystems around the world through research and education, science and technology, and advocacy." The Institute has several programs; forestry is the one of which Arnosti is the Director.

Arnosti briefly explains their Forestry Program. "We collaborate with landowners, forestry cooperatives, and conservation organizations to ensure sustainable land management. Our challenge is to make responsible forestry work for private landowners and their communities."

In 1909, President Teddy Roosevelt established the Superior National Forest. This 3-million-acre forest is located in northeastern Minnesota, is the eighth most visited national forest in our country, and is known worldwide for its Boundary Waters Canoe Area Wilderness.

The Superior National Forest is a natural fire-prone forest. As a result of decades of fire suppression and fuel accumulation, large areas of the forest are at risk of "stand replacing" crown fires. During the past 2 years, the forest has experienced the two largest such fires in its recent history in an area of blown-down timber.

All of this forest has been classified by the Forest Service as either Condition Class 2 or 3, which means that these areas have departed from their historical fire regimes and can present persistent wildland fire problems. Currently, three Community Wildfire Protection Plans are being prepared that identify large areas (660,000 acres) as high fire hazard and risk due to fuel loads and poor access. Much of the area is in the rapidly growing wildland–urban interface and is considered as a top priority for forest fuel treatments.

The specific purpose of the National Woody Biomass Utilization grant to Arnosti and his partners was to conduct test biomass harvests on fire-prone lands of the Superior National Forest. A study was designed to understand the economic and operational barriers as well as the impact on forest resources of such harvests.

Arnosti explained that two key barriers currently hinder removal of woody biomass from the Superior National Forest. "The first barrier is that many in the logging business had not previously cut woody biomass material and are unfamiliar with the operating conditions. They were concerned about compatibility of their equipment, and

Woody biomass bundles (Source: IATP)

possibly the unknown cost of cutting non-commercial timber."

The second key barrier is "the inefficiency of completing environmental assessments on prescribed woody biomass removals from national forest sites due to present shortcomings of local best management practices (BMPs), which were developed without considering woody biomass removals from the forest."

According to Arnosti, the BMPs need to be updated to specifically consider not only the removal of tree trunks, tops, and limbs, but also efforts that specifically target small-diameter trees and brush in the understory.

The three partners with IATP on this woody biomass grant project are the Superior National Forest, the Laurentian Energy Authority (LEA), and Forest Management Systems, a cooperative logging business.

The plan for this project was thoroughly laid out. Nine test biomass harvests were conducted

Institute for Agriculture and Trade Policy
2105 First Avenue South
Minneapolis, MN 55404

Bundler (Source: IATP)

Loose woody biomass material (Source: IATP)

on more than 100 acres of sites on the Superior National Forest identified in Community Wildfire Protection Plans. Little of the woody biomass material from these sites had any commercial timber value. Sites were selected in areas of insect-killed balsam and where understory trees provided dense "ladder fuel" from the ground to the forest crown. Various harvesting equipment and techniques were tested. The project partners collected and analyzed environmental, cost, and productivity data for each test site and made this information available to the public.

IATP served as the Project Coordinator and was responsible for, among other things, accurate reporting, making sure all parts of the project functioned together and on time, coordinating data to design ecological and monitoring components, and ensuring the results of the study would be published and made public.

Forest Service personnel from the Superior National Forest identified the high-priority sites for test harvests,

coordinated National Environmental Policy Act (NEPA) and related analysis and procedures, and ensured that the woody biomass removal was performed properly.

Forest Management Systems and other area loggers did the actual harvesting. They identified and researched a variety of equipment and harvest techniques, trained operators, and are now helping to educate the logging community about the results of the project.

Laurentian Energy Authority loaned the grinder, purchased the woody biomass harvested from the test sites, and is also helping to publicize the results of this project. (LEA is a partnership of the Public Utilities of Virginia and Hibbing, Minnesota, which operate wood-fueled district heating and electrical generation facilities in these communities.)

This study was originally designed to provide information to address two sets of barriers. However, Arnosti said, "In the course of our study, we determined that administrative issues and constraints formed a third barrier to the development of biomass markets. Although no definitive right way to harvest biomass for energy use can be identified as a result of these trials, important information was uncovered that is of value to land managers as they consider the use of biomass harvest as a tool to achieve their desired land management goals."

The following, provided by Arnosti, presents only a few of the recommendations as a result of this study regarding key barriers that can hinder removal of woody biomass. For a complete project report, please contact Arnosti through IATP.

Administrative Issues

- Biomass management activities must be considered and incorporated at early phases of the planning process.

- Site prescriptions tailored to the practical and operational needs of biomass harvest are critical. When possible, these should be flexible prescriptions that allow operator-determined options to lay out skid trails, reserve areas, and permit a minimal removal of residual trees to facilitate harvest and forwarding.

- Combining roundwood and biomass harvest is one strategy to improve on-site maneuverability and harvest efficiency.

- Clear site demarcation can speed up operations.

- Minimize forwarding distance to biomass yarding areas.

- Plan landings of sufficient size to accommodate all harvested biomass.

- Focus biomass removals on larger materials and high-density areas.

- Emphasize communication and coordination between the forest managers and operators early in the planning.

- Communicating to operators why certain prescriptions require specific exclusions or restrictions promotes an informed understanding of the harvesting goals.

Harvest, Forwarding, and Processing Equipment and Techniques

- Efficient layout of harvest access trails reduces harvest and forwarding time.

- Equipment should be selected that is suitable to the terrain and forest conditions.

- Less expensive equipment (such as biomass processing heads in place of timber processing heads) can improve harvest economics.

- Learning the techniques necessary to search, harvest, and recover smaller biomass material will lead to improved efficiency and cost reductions.

- Forwarding of materials should take place right after material is cut to improve speed and total recovery of material.

- Forwarding and bundling hours can be reduced if material is sized and arranged in organized piles.

- Adaptations to standard forwarding equipment are not necessary for biomass; however, operators need to learn new techniques of loading and maneuvering to be successful.

- Bundling of biomass, although feasible, results in additional costs for the harvester, which must be rewarded with a superior price at the biomass market.

- Self-loading grinders should be used to eliminate the need for a separate loader.

Environmental Considerations

- Materials less than 1 inch in dbh (diameter at breast height) contained a small percentage of the total volume of biomass.

- On our test sites, materials from 1 to 5 inches dbh generally held far more volume than smaller materials and were a significant source of biomass.

- The highest harvest removal in these trials was 75% of the stems less than 1-inch dbh and 94% of stems greater than 1-inch dbh. Most sites fell well under this level of harvest.

- Snags were far less impacted by the harvesting activity than expected.

Loading trucks (Source: IATP)

Harvester (Source: IATP)

Market Considerations

- Distance to biomass markets should be no greater than 100 miles, preferably considerably less.

- Payment should be per ton and adjusted for moisture content to reward on-site drying and to transport dryer, more favorable materials.

- If bundles are desired for biomass storage reasons, payment must reflect this value.

Montana Community Development Corp.

The need for hazardous forest fuel reduction has reached critical levels in Montana. According to State Forester Bob Harrington, "more than 80% of the 22.5 million acres of Montana forested land is at a high or moderate risk from damaging wildfires or insect and disease infestation."

However, forest fuel reduction treatment results in large quantities of woody biomass or slash left in the woods. Slash is the material (tops and limbs) left over when trees are thinned during forest restoration. Slash is either scattered or piled in the forest but this can also create a fire hazard. What do you do with 2 million tons of slash that is left each year at logging sites in Montana?

Slash material is considered very low in value, is not economical to transport, and can cause pollution problems if burned. However, slash can be ground into chips and transported to co-generation facilities and used as fuel to heat boilers.

Craig Rawlings, Small Wood Enterprise Agent of Montana Community Development Corporation (MCDC), agrees that burning slash in the forest is not the best answer. He believes that a good solution is the Woody Biomass Collection System, an economical alternative to burning and mechanical methods of handling slash. The Collection System involves a network of partners helping to solve the slash problem.

The MCDC, located in Missoula, Montana, is a nonprofit organization with 20 years of experience in business financing, project development, and business technical assistance, especially in the area of small-wood innovations.

According to Rawlings, in 2004 several agencies and MCDC brought Canadian containers and related machinery to Montana to conduct field trials and complete extensive cost analyses to determine the feasibility of collecting and transporting slash and to compare bin transport options with conventional hauling.

Private businesses invested in these trials by contributing money, equipment, and time. Several roll-on/roll-off containers were filled in the forested areas with slash and then hauled to a collection yard. At the yard, materials were combined and sold at the highest market value. Based on these field trials, the potential to expand this container technology was deemed very high.

"The trials also showed a direct savings to the federal government of $35–50 per acre when this collection system is substituted for burn treatment on federal land," said Rawlings.

Montana Community
    Development Corporation
110 East Broadway #200
Missoula, MT 59802

Roll-on/roll-off container placed in fuel reduction site

Utilization grant, the Collection System was then able to organize, equip, and address slash removal by developing an economical way to collect, transport, and sell it for profit. In due course, the Collection System plans to also handle removal of urban wood waste, wooden pallets, clean construction debris, and both merchantable and unmerchantable logs that are harvested in less than truck-load quantities.

The MCDC is the project leader on this project and coordinates all work. Those that have committed to this project include All Woody Resources, Horizon Tree Service, Fire Solutions, the Bitterroot Resource

Based on their findings and with the help of a U.S. Forest Service National Woody Biomass

Woody biomass being loaded onto container

Truck and trailer transporting small-diameter logs— Roll-on/roll-off refers to a straight frame tractor and pup trailer configuration in which modular containers are "rolled" onto and off of the straight frame tractor (commonly referred to as a "Hook Truck") and the pup trailer, by means of a tractor-mounted hydraulic grapple. (A pup trailer is a four-axle trailer towed by the hook truck.)

Truck loading roll-on/roll-off container.

Roll-on/roll-off rack for transporting logs

Conservation & Development (RC&D) Council, and the University of Montana, School of Forestry. Currently, most of the forest fire reduction projects that the Collection System is working on are located on the Lolo and Bitterroot National Forests.

All Woody Resources operates and promotes the collection system. It developed the central collection yard, makes available the roll-on/roll-off containers, and provides partial staffing at the collection yard. All Woody Resources also provides a hook truck, trailer, and loader for container transport and service. This company contributes through their logging and hazardous fuel reduction services. Horizon Tree Service and Fire Solutions also provide logging and hazardous fuel reduction services and participates, especially in the wildland–urban interface areas. The Bitterroot RC&D Council cost-shares 700 to 800 acres of fuel reduction projects each year and plays a big role in the Collection System through their outreach and education efforts. The University of Montana, School of Forestry, collects data on this project for possible replication in other areas.

Rawlings explained how the Collection System operates. "We have a central yard with eight log bunks and nine slash bins (roll-on/roll-off containers); up to four containers always remain at the collection yard. The containers are transported to the job sites of various private logging and forestry companies. These companies use the containers to collect slash at the job site, then the full containers are transported to the central yard. There, slash from around the region is aggregated and sorted so that it can be sold for its highest value." He added, "We also hope to attract maximum use of the central yard by residential and municipal customers."

Roll-on/roll-off containers make slash totally accessible because the trucks that carry them can navigate the narrow and windy mountainous roads where many of the fuel reduction sites are located. In addition to the roll-on/roll-off containers, a hook truck and trailer for transport and a loader are needed.

Craig Thomas, Vice President of All Woody Resources, fabricated the roll-on/roll-off containers. Some hold 44 cubic yards of material, and some can hold 58 cubic yards. The containers are slightly wider on the bottom and slightly wider in the back. To provide for easy storage and transport, the containers fit inside each other, similar to the way paper cups stack up. Also, the loader can be handily stored on site inside these containers.

When asked about the future of this project, Rawlings said "I believe this project will change a part of the timber harvesting industry. The Collection System can be easily adapted to any area, especially where there is a lot of forest fuel reduction work going on. It will provide opportunities for value-added products, help create jobs, and contribute to healthy forest management."

Some consider the pocosin ecosystem to include one of the most flammable vegetation types in the U.S. South. To help reduce these hazardous fuel conditions, Dr. Joseph Roise, professor of forest management operations at North Carolina State University, is working to develop an efficient machine that would swath-harvest woody biomass from pocosins.

Pocosins are evergreen shrub- and tree-dominated landscapes found on the Atlantic Coastal Plain from Virginia to northern Florida, although most are found in North Carolina. The word pocosin comes from the Native American word for "swamp on a hill." Usually, no standing water is present in pocosins, but a shallow water table leaves the soil saturated for much of the year. Pocosins range in size from less than an acre to several thousand acres.

On the Croatan National Forest and in many southern states, wildfire suppression activities over the past 60 years have allowed a large build-up of woody biomass on almost all forestlands, including pocosin ecosystems. The only safe way to reduce these fuel loads is by mechanical removal. However, current mechanical treatments can cost between $500 and $1,200 per acre. Mulching is also expensive, and prescribed fire is too dangerous to apply with such high fuel loading, especially in the wildland–urban interface areas.

According to Roise, "If this small-diameter (less than 6-inch diameter) woody biomass material could to be harvested by machine and sold to produce feedstock for energy production for less than the current rate of $500 per acre, it would spread the hazardous fuel reduction dollars over more acres."

Close up of the head on experimental harvester

Department of Forestry
and Environmental Resources
North Carolina State University
Raleigh, NC 27695

A pocosin, showing type of woody biomass material that needs harvesting, in an urban–wildland interface area on the Croatan National Forest

Experimental harvester in operation

FECON, Inc., had been working on a harvesting machine designed to collect woody biomass but had not manufactured or tested the design. After discussions with Dr. Roise at North Carolina State University, a project was laid out to manufacture, test, refine, demonstrate, utilize, and ultimately promote a redesign of the mulching head into a harvest and collection system that would efficiently harvest small-diameter woody biomass. It was decided that a good test for this prototype would be on Croatan National Forest acres that desperately needed fuel reduction in the wildland–urban interface.

In 2006, Dr. Roise applied for and received a National Woody Biomass Utilization Grant from the U.S. Forest Service to assist in his project to create a biomass harvesting machine by redesigning the mulching head into a harvesting head and collection system.

Many partners are involved in this experimental biomass harvester project. FECON, Inc., is providing the new head design, manufacturing, refinements, and operating expertise needed. The Croatan National Forest is providing access to acres needed to harvest woody biomass in addition to helping with equipment whenever needed. Craven

Dumping the woody biomass material for pickup

Machine operator Tim Tabak, Resource Manager/Consultant, Association of Consulting Foresters, New Bern, North Carolina, standing next to harvester head

Wood Energy, a 45-megawatt electric generating plant in New Bern, North Carolina, is supplying the market for the harvested woody biomass, helping to test the biomass fuel properties, and providing logistical support including transportation. The North Carolina Forestry Foundation is providing access to their machine shop, staff support, equipment, and living arrangements for project personnel.

The experimental harvester weighs 56,000 pounds and is pushed by a 440-horsepower engine tractor on treads. It produces a ground pressure of only 7.1 pounds per square foot, so it moves through the brush easily over the soft forest bed and pocosin. As it moves along, the harvester cuts a trail with carbide teeth and pulverizes the biomass in its 6-foot-wide path. A belt-driven vacuum sucks the cuttings back though a chute and into an agricultural wagon that is hooked to the tractor. When the wagon is full, it is dumped into a bin for later pickup. Each time the wagon is dumped, the contents are weighed to measure productivity.

According to Roise, the machine can now harvest between 2 and 4 tons of woody biomass material per hour. "The machine can harvest anything in its path but is most productive with 1- to 2-inch material." However, the machine needs to harvest about 10 tons per hour to break even. "Our ultimate goal is for a small business to operate one of these machines at a profit."

"In 4 or 5 years the biomass harvester will be commonly used in the renewable biomass energy/hazardous fuel reduction business. FECON is currently working on the next generation harvesting head, and refinements to the material collection and transportation system are underway. We will be doing 10 tons per hour by this time next year," said Roise.

Other uses for this equipment, when perfected, could be plantation thinning in tree farming, clearing between rows, and forest management.

Roise said their next move is to continue working on the machine's productivity rate. They are concentrating on

Dr. Joseph Roise, professor of forest management operations at North Carolina State University

density and material size right now. Stem density in the pocosins commonly ranges from 6,000 to 12,000 per acre. "We know what the improvements need to be—FECON is already working on making the improvements and we are excited about the next design."

"We are getting close to being able to cover all production and transportation costs with the sale of harvested biomass. This would surely be an incentive toward timely wildfire fuel reduction activities," concluded Roise.

Northern Nevada Correctional Center

On September 4, 2007, I attended a ribbon-cutting ceremony for a woody biomass renewable energy, 1-megawatt combined heat and power plant at the Northern Nevada Correctional Center (NNCC), located just outside Carson City, Nevada. This Renewable Energy Center is believed to the first of its kind in the state and will save millions of dollars in energy costs over the next several years.

NNCC's Renewable Energy Center includes a 1-megawatt steam turbine generater. One megawatt is enough power for the electrical needs of 500 average-sized homes in northern Nevada. This heat and power plant efficiently burns woody biomass from forest restoration projects to produce the electricity, steam, and hot water for 1,500 inmates at the Carson City NNCC.

Founded in 1858, Carson City is named after the famous frontiersman and scout "Kit" Carson. Surrounding the area are U.S. Forest Service lands including the Eldorado and the Humboldt–Toiyabe National Forests and the Lake Tahoe Basin Management Unit. The Eldorado National Forest is located in the central Sierra Nevada Mountains. The Humboldt–Toiyabe National Forest encompasses all of Nevada and the far eastern edge of California. The Humboldt–Toiyabe is the largest forest in the lower 48 states, having 10 ranger districts to manage the acreage. The Lake Tahoe Basin Management Unit encompasses more than 150,000 acres of National Forest lands that overlook the city of South Lake Tahoe.

The NNCC has received several grants since the inception of this project. Directed by the Nevada Fire Safe Council, the Forest Service/Nevada State Economic Development group funded a $50,000 study of biomass potential in the Carson area. Carson City helped to develop a site for woody biomass processing next to the landfill with a $20,000 grant from the U.S. Forest Service Rural Community Assistance Program. In 2005, the NNCC received a $250,000 grant from the U.S. Forest Service for assistance in creating the Renewable Energy Center.

Projections are that this heat and power plant will save the facility and state more than $9 million in energy costs over the next 20 years. Excess energy will be sold to Sierra Pacific Power Co., which will also provide some revenue to NNCC. The Renewable Energy Center also includes 30 kilowatts of solar (photovoltaic) power located on the roof.

Lori Bagwell, Chief of Fiscal Services for NNCC, invested an enormous amount of time pulling this project together. She said "This project works on every level. Not only do we expect air and water quality in the area to be improved by the way we are now handling the

Northern Nevada
Correctional Center
P.O. Box 7011
Carson City, NV 89702

Sign outside correctional facility

Lori Bagwell, Chief of Fiscal Services, cutting ribbon at ceremony

disposal of woody biomass but we will see huge utility savings at NNCC."

Bagwell says fuel requirements for the plant are estimated at about 17,000 tons per year and are being supplied by Carson City Renewable Resources. Although the majority of these fuels currently come from waste wood in the city's landfill, as more infrastructure is created in the area, more material will come from hazardous fuel reduction projects on the national forests.

Successfully completing this project required a host of partners from both the public and private arenas.

According to Ed Monnig, Forest Supervisor on the Humboldt–Toiyabe National Forest, "Grants along with the work of many dedicated local, state, and federal partners in both the private and public sector culminated in an $8.3 million investment on the part of the State of Nevada in this energy project. We are all committed to this facility and to doing what we can to ensure its success."

APS Energy Services, the general contractor, was responsible for the analysis, design, and construction of the NNCC facility. APS Energy Services is a full-service energy services provider based out of Arizona.

The Bureau of Land Management (BLM) made 43 acres available to Carson City next to the landfill for a biomass staging and processing site. Carson City Renewable Resources removes the biomass from forest thinning operations and delivers it to NNCC. The Nevada Division of Forestry and the U.S. Forest Service work in harmony to provide information on the availability of woody biomass.

Monnig summed up the success of this project when he spoke at the ceremony. "This is an amazing story of persistence and cooperation interspersed with occasional false starts, miscommunications, and organizational challenges. In the end, the cooperative spirit prevailed. We salute the efforts of several agencies and all partners in bringing this facility to reality."

Ed Monnig, Forest Supervisor on the Humboldt–Toiyabe National Forest

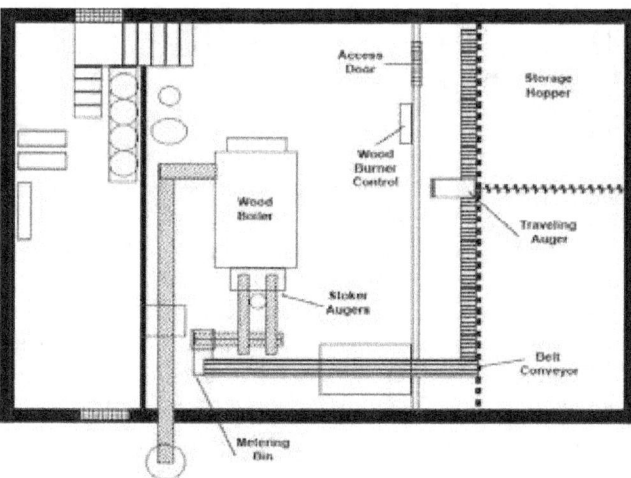

Layout of energy facility

REACH, Incorporated

REACH is a special company in a special community. Its motto is "Sustaining People, Communities and the Earth," which gives you some insight into this company. REACH offers employment that provides experience and training for people with disabilities.

Organized in the early 1980s, REACH, Incorporated, stands for Restoration, Education and Community Habilitation. The company is located in Klamath Falls, Oregon, which has a population of about 42,000 and is located in the south central region of Oregon, nestled in the eastern slopes of the Cascade Mountains.

In 1998, the Klamath Falls community of ranchers, farmers, environmentalists, governments, and others came together to try to solve their problem of the invasive western juniper. Part of their solution was to contact REACH to help develop and manufacture value-added products made from this species.

Over the past 150 years, western juniper (*Juniperus occidentalis*) has increased almost tenfold. Juniper outcompetes other vegetation for water and poses a threat to watersheds and ecosystem health. Until REACH's involvement, juniper had little value as a product except for fence posts and firewood. Juniper is also expensive to harvest because it is short and extremely tapered and has a very dense limb structure.

In contrast, positive traits of western juniper include its high durable and aromatic scent, similar to that of cedar. The wood is resistant to decay and insects; it is dense, hard, and machines, glues, and finishes well. When dried, juniper shrinks and swells less than other Pacific Northwest species. It is considered to be one of the hardest softwoods.

Upon accepting the challenge, REACH began receiving the salvage from western juniper forest restoration projects in the area. After 9 years of work and experience, REACH employees have developed and now manufacture a variety of value-added products from western juniper. REACH has 12 employees dedicated to the juniper project. In other local manufacturing companies, most of these employees would have significant challenges finding work.

"The more wood mill jobs we have the better job we can do of matching skills to employees. That's what this is all about—the people—that's why we are here," said Toby Loetscher, Production Manufacturing Director and Special Projects Manager.

REACH, Incorporated
2350 Maywood Drive
P.O. Box 1089
Klamath Falls, OR 97601

As a donated executive from a local land holding company, JWTR, LLC, Toby enthusiastically runs the juniper portion of the REACH mill.

Toby Loetscher (center), of REACH, and Mike Bechdolt (left) and Terry Fairbanks (right), both from the Bureau of Land Management, beside pallets made by REACH

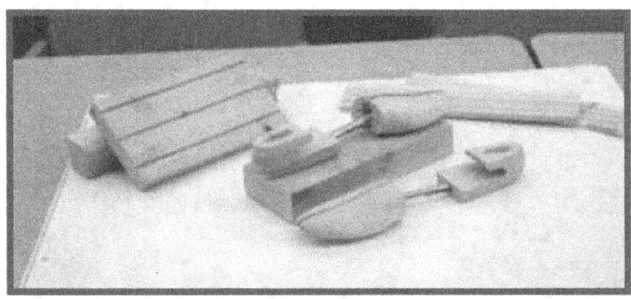

Decking material, paneling, and 2- by 4-inch kiln-dried cutstock blocks shaped into an aromatic shoe tree

The REACH mill is staffed with about 90 employees, and roughly 80% of their sales volume is from non-juniper products, such as pallets and dimension lumber, which are made from pine or fir. The mill also has a state-of-the-art dehumidification dry kiln and does some custom drying of other species.

Initially, REACH's only juniper product was animal bedding. Their line of products now includes pre-finished engineered flooring, rough-cut flooring, tongue-and-groove paneling, decking material, 4- by 4- inch to 8- by 8-inch posts 8 to 10 feet in length, fence boards, peeled and doweled poles, and 2- by 4-inch kiln-dried cutstock blocks. These juniper blocks are made from the waste from other products. The blocks are shipped to China, shaped into an aromatic shoe tree, and sold in Japan and some European countries.

Toby says their biggest problem is supply. "We are lucky to get two or three truck loads of juniper from a large logging operation in one day. It's just flat out hard to work with, hard on the chain saw, and hard on the equipment."

REACH has both small- and large-diameter mills. Twelve-inch diameter material is the largest that their small-diameter mill can handle. For the non-juniper mill, they

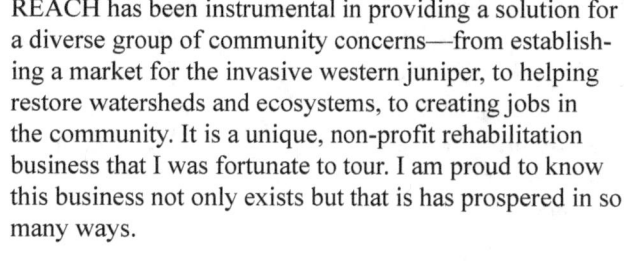

Truck load of juniper supply being delivered to yard

REACH has been instrumental in providing a solution for a diverse group of community concerns—from establishing a market for the invasive western juniper, to helping restore watersheds and ecosystems, to creating jobs in the community. It is a unique, non-profit rehabilitation business that I was fortunate to tour. I am proud to know this business not only exists but that is has prospered in so many ways.

Juniper supply in yard

run one 8-hour shift, five days per week. In their juniper mill, they have two 10-hour shifts, 4 days per week. On a good day, they can run six log trucks through the mill.

Toby figures that one log truck is the equivalent of about 2,000 board feet of solid lumber. "We process anywhere from 10,000 to 12,000 board feet per day." Toby recounts the following breakdown from juniper logs: "For every 1,000 pounds of logs that come into REACH, 650 pounds become chips for a local fiber plant that is making a 1/8-inch-thick skin for a hollow-core interior door, and 150 pounds are fines for hog fuel. The remaining 20%, or 200 pounds, are processed in our mill into posts and kiln-dried products."

About 90% of REACH's non-juniper products are sold to three businesses, all within the Klamath Falls area: Columbia Plywood Corp., Collins Products LLC (particleboard), and JELD-WEN Windows & Doors. Toby notes that most of their pallet and packaging products are custom made for the client.

Rough & Ready Lumber Co.

Link and Jennifer Phillippi, owners of the Rough & Ready Lumber Co., have found a positive way to connect wood waste with their energy needs.

Rough & Ready is a third-generation sawmill and lumber manufacturing business located about 4 miles south of Cave Junction, Oregon. It has been in operation for 84 years.

Cave Junction is a small town of about 2,500 and is considered the "Gateway to the Oregon Caves National Monument." In a rural community made up of small farms, woodlots, craft people, and families, Cave Junction is nestled in the Siskiyous Mountains—about half-way to the Oregon Coast. Seventy percent of the forests in this area are managed by either the U.S. Forest Service or the Bureau of Land Management (BLM).

Rough & Ready is a traditional cutting sawmill. In other words, the majority of its fir and pine lumber products are cut to order and sold to remanufacturers for doors, windows, and other specified cuttings. These products are distributed throughout the United States, Japan, and Europe.

As a well-established company, most of the bottlenecks within Rough & Ready have been worked out. After 84 years of providing good service and quality products, its customer base is almost unshakable. It is also one of the largest, most dependable businesses in the area, with about 85 full-time employees.

Link noted that although they have two sawmills on site, one for large-diameter logs and one for small-diameter logs, their current supply dictates running only one sawmill at a time and one shift. He wishes they had enough supply for both sawmills and another shift.

Supply has been a problem for the past 10 years. Link says "We struggle to find logs. We used to get about 90% of our supply from federal lands. Now it is almost zero percent. We haven't been able to buy a federal timber contract since 1997. Right now two of our BLM contracts are tied up in litigation."

Due to the unknown quantity of supply and in order to continue operation, over the years Rough & Ready has purchased and manages 30,000 acres of timber.

Their most recent project is building a steam-generated power plant at their facility that is fueled by wood and capable of providing 1.5 megawatts of energy.

Link says "We wanted to build a woody biomass power facility to be in balance with our operation. In 4 years, we expect the project to pay back its cost in energy savings."

Rough & Ready Lumber Co.
30365 Redwood Highway
Cave Junction, OR 97523

Jennifer and Link Phillippi

Lumber ready for transport

The new boiler and turbine will produce enough combined power and heat to operate the two sawmills, eight existing dry kilns, and the four new dry kilns that the company is in the process of building.

"We feel drying is a value-added part of our business. Most of the market demands dry lumber," commented Link.

Both Energy Trust of Oregon, Inc., a nonprofit organization that promotes energy efficiency and clean, renewable energy, and the U.S. Forest Service, through their National Woody Biomass Utilization Grant Program, have helped with the new boiler/turbine system by providing dollars to ease the financial burden on Rough & Ready. The total cost of Rough & Ready's project is about $5.4 million.

The new boiler/turbine system requires 30,000 bone dry tons (BDT) of wood per year. Rough & Ready has plenty of wood residuals on hand for burning—at least 15,000 BDT per year. The remaining 15,000 BDT will be collected from fuels treatment and thinning projects from nearby Forest Service, BLM, and other lands. This woody biomass material will be burned in the mill's upgraded boiler system to produce process steam for their dry kilns and generate electrical power. At present, they have a signed interconnect agreement and will soon finalize

Wood-fueled steam-generated power plant

additional documents so that electrical power can be sold to their public utility.

Rough & Ready has had a few problems along the way with the installation of the new boiler/turbine system. Although their plan has been delayed by at least a month, Link said they are now operational and on-grid with their public utility.

Link modestly said, "We could not have afforded to build this without the financial and technology assistance from so many. We are proud that we are going to be producing clean renewable energy and at the same time contributing to the health of southwestern Oregon's forests."

This community is fortunate to have creative and forward-thinking members like Link and Jennifer Phillippi from Rough & Ready Lumber Co., who I am confident will continue to serve their community well.

Bureau of Land Management and Stewardship Contracting

Contrary to what some people assume, the U.S. Forest Service does not manage all federally held forest lands.

In 1905, Congress established the Forest Service to provide quality water and timber for the Nation's benefit. Over time, Congress and the public have directed the Forest Service to manage national forests for additional multiple uses and benefits and for the sustainability of renewable resources such as water, forage, wildlife, wood, and recreation. Today, the Forest Service encompasses 193 million acres, with 155 national forests and 20 grasslands.

The Bureau of Land Management (BLM) was established in 1946 and is responsible for a variety of programs on approximately 958 million acres of both surface lands and subsurface mineral resources, located primarily in 12 western states. Included in these acres are about 57 million acres of forests and woodlands.

The BLM and U.S. Forest Service have common fire management missions and work cooperatively to administer numerous federal programs.

BLM History

The history leading to the establishment of the BLM is an interesting chronicle. In the 1700s, only "Ordinances" existed to provide guidance for the survey and settlement of the lands that the original 13 colonies ceded to the Federal government after the War of Independence. As additional territories were acquired, Congress directed that these lands be explored, surveyed, and made available for settlement.

In 1812, Congress established the General Land Office to oversee the disposition of these Federal lands. However, in the late 19th century, priorities shifted and the first national parks, forests, and wildlife refuges were created. The U.S. Congress made the decision not only to promote private settlement on public lands but also to hold some of these lands in public ownership.

Over the years, several Federal Acts were passed to allow leasing and the production of coal, oil, and gas and to manage these public rangelands and timberlands. It wasn't until 1946 that the U.S. Congress established the BLM as an agency within the U.S. Department of Interior; it was

BLM Stewardship Contracting
(Source: Western Forester, Sept/Oct. 2006, vol. 51, no. 5, Society of American Foresters)

Until September 30, 2013, the U.S. Forest Service and BLM have the authority to enter into stewardship projects with private persons or public or private entities by contract or agreement to perform services to achieve land management objectives for the national forests or public lands that meet local and rural community needs.

- Stewardship contracting is not a replacement for the established timber sale program. Forest management projects designed primarily to enhance volume are not suitable for stewardship contracts.

- Stewardship projects shall comply with applicable environmental laws and regulations, including the appropriate level of environmental review under the National Environmental Policy Act (NEPA) and are consistent with the applicable land use plans.

- Any vegetative material removal must be a byproduct of meeting the stewardship contracting project goals. Removal of these products must be consistent with the objectives developed through the collaborative process and the applicable land use plan objectives.

- Stewardship contracting projects involve treatments and techniques to make forests, woodlands, and rangelands more resilient to natural disturbances such as fire, insects, disease, wind, and flood.

For contracts exceeding 5 years in duration, field managers consider such factors as scope of the project, type of the material to be treated, availability of local capacity to process and use the material removed from the land, and potential development of new markets for small-diameter material, as well as operational factors such as local weather patterns, sensitive wildlife species, habitat use cycles, and seasonal restrictions for wildfire prevention.

a consolidation of the General Land Office and Grazing Service.

Until 1976 and the passage of the Federal Land Policy and Management Act (FLPMA), the BLM had no unified laws to manage these public lands. In FLPMA, Congress not only declared that these lands would continue to be owned by all Americans but they gave us the term "multiple use" management, defined as "management of the public lands and their various resource values so that they are utilized in the combination that will best meet the present and future needs of the American people."

BLM Today

In 2007, the BLM managed 258 million acres of surface land and approximately 700 million acres of subsurface mineral resources. Most BLM-managed lands are located in the western United States and Alaska and are dominated by extensive grasslands, forests, high mountains, arctic tundra, and deserts. These public lands provide significant economic benefits to our Nation and to states and counties where these lands are located. Income generated from public lands makes BLM one of the top revenue-generating agencies in the Federal government.

BLM manages a wide variety of resources and uses, including energy and minerals; timber; forage; wild horse and burro populations; fish and wildlife habitat; wilderness areas; archaeological, paleontological, and historical sites; and other natural heritage values.

In the Pacific Northwest, Fire and Aviation Management is managed cooperatively between the BLM and the U.S. Forest Service. This interagency authority covers both Oregon and Washington and includes 10 BLM districts, 19 National Forests, and the Columbia Gorge National Scenic Area.

In western Oregon, the BLM manages 2 million acres of forest in a checkerboard ownership pattern. These forests provide important habitat for many threatened and endangered fish and wildlife species and are considered some of the most productive forests in the world.

The BLM and U.S. Forest Service have common fire management missions and objectives. They cooperatively administer fire, fuels, and aviation programs in a manner that eliminates duplication, increases program efficiency, and capitalizes on the expertise of each agency's personnel. In 2003, both BLM and the Forest Service received authority to enter into long-term stewardship contracts (see sidebar on BLM Stewardship Contracting).

Stewardship contracting is an important tool that is available to both the Forest Service and BLM to aid in the increased utilization of small-diameter and woody biomass material. BLM stewardship contracts are a little different in the particulars from Forest Service stewardship contracts. However, both BLM and the Forest Service stewardship contracts have the same objectives.

BLM Stewardship Contracting

In 2003, the Consolidated Appropriations Resolution was signed, giving authority to BLM and the Forest Service to enter into long-term stewardship contracts.

According to Mike Bechdolt, Lead Forester and Timber Manager from the BLM Lakeview District, since receiving this authority, Washington and Oregon BLM offices have awarded 24 stewardship contracts. These contracts

involve restoration treatments such as streamside habitat enhancement, fish habitat improvement, biomass utilization for energy production, precommercial thinning, fence construction wildlife habitat improvement, and hazardous fuel reduction.

Two of southwestern BLM's successful stewardship contracts include the "Gerber" in the Lakeview District and "Penny" in the Medford District.

Gerber Stewardship Project: The Gerber Stewardship contract was awarded in September 2004. The objective was to treat 10,000 acres over a period of 10 years. The Gerber project is located in southern Oregon near Klamath Falls.

Bechdolt said the purpose and design of the initial contract and treatments were to experiment with the restoration and utilization markets for western juniper. "As part of the National Fire Plan, from 1997 through 2005, the Klamath Falls Resource Area had treated more than 20,000 acres of rangelands and western juniper woodlands, primarily cutting and burning the western juniper as a rangeland restoration treatment. Up until 2003, when the Stewardship Authority was received, less than 500 acres of western juniper had been utilized by local wood products facilities. The expanding and increasing local demand for western juniper and increasing use in lieu of burning was the primary impetus for the design of the Gerber Stewardship contract in 2004. The design of the stewardship contract quickly expanded when additional funding became available to treat additional lands for forest health needs and hazard fuel reduction purposes."

Two aspects of the stewardship contracts, says Bechdolt, are that it (1) authorizes the value of vegetative material to be applied as an offset against the costs of services received and (2) allows multi-year contract authority up to 10 years. Neither of these authorities is available under standard BLM timber sales or service contracts.

The Gerber Stewardship contract was set up as an Indefinite Delivery/Indefinite Quantity (ID/IQ) contract. This type of contract specifies minimum and maximum quantities of services and products and allows the government to place task orders against the base contract. This means individual treatments such as cutting, yarding, and removal of juniper; manual cutting and piling of juniper around sensitive spring sites; road resurfacing; fencing; seeding; removal of residual landing slash for biomass; and slashbusting can be requested through task orders. The benefit to the government is that additional work can be accomplished as funding becomes available, and the benefit to the contractor is the opportunity to bid on a long-term contract.

In the Gerber Stewardship contract, the cost of the service work exceeded the value of the product removed.

Bureau of Land Management stewardship contracts in progress.

However, Bechdolt says that this is not always the case with stewardship contracts. It all depends on the amount of commercial sawlog material included in the contract and how much service work is involved.

Another aspect noted by Bechdolt is the challenge that it presents to contractors when bidding on stewardship contracts. The contractor takes a big risk when bidding on multiple types of treatments, not knowing the amount of income that will be realized from the material and the challenges, changes, or modifications that could occur over the life of a 10-year contract, including fluctuating forest product markets. Allowances need to be built into the contracts, which has posed a challenge for all.

Bechdolt says that the "Gerber Stewardship contract is considered successful because it is providing employment in rural communities, meeting restoration goals, building utilization markets, and reducing wildfire risks." He also feels that "these contracts encourage long-term commitments and stability between the government, the contractors, and the community. BLM and the contractors are learning to adapt as each treatment is implemented and new stewardship contracts are awarded."

Penny Stewardship Project: I interviewed Terry Fairbanks, BLM Oregon/Washington Stewardship & Biomass Coordinator for information on the Penny Stewardship contract.

The Penny Stewardship project was also awarded in 2004. The project is located in the Applegate Valley, near Williams, Oregon, and initially included 100 acres of commercial and precommercial thinning, brushing, and fuels hazard reduction work.

The project area was officially listed as a community at risk under the National Fire Plan, and there was strong community interest in developing strategies that would facilitate economic and recreational opportunities in the Williams community.

Located in the rural wildland–urban interface, the project objectives were to (1) improve stand vigor, including resistance to insect and disease in Douglas-fir and ponderosa pine stands, and (2) reduce hazardous fuels by thinning understory conifers, shrubs, and hardwood trees.

The BLM held a variety of meetings with local community groups and small businesses who were interested in participating in small project and utilization activities in the Williams Watershed.

For example, the local watershed council was involved in several meetings to discuss this project. Small businesses and local individuals evaluated the project, became familiar with stewardship projects, and were interested in bidding on this project. A couple of organizations were interested in job development opportunities and met with

BLM to discuss this project. More than 20 people attended the pre-bid meeting.

The Penny Stewardship project was purposefully designed to test the ability to market small-diameter material, gain acceptance by the environmental community, and provide hazardous fuel reduction near rural homes while maintaining aesthetic values.

The contractor was required to demonstrate in their proposal an awareness of local uses and values, the ability to market material locally, the skills to meet fuel model and condition class ratings through the development of site-specific prescriptions, and the ability to conduct public meetings and field trips.

An unused BLM maintenance yard was made available for the contractor to use as a sort yard. Products resulting from the project included post and poles, teepee poles, saw logs, fire wood, and biomass.

This stewardship project, although small, was determined to be successful for the following reasons:

- Widespread acceptance was gained for the types of treatments that were included in the contract.

- Four new stewardship projects that are much larger and can extend up to 10 years were awarded in the adjacent valley.

- Initial skepticism by contractors has been overcome and new contractors are coming forward to bid on the projects.

- The local environmental community is involved in several collaborative efforts to promote small-wood development.

After interviewing Bechdolt and Fairbanks, I interviewed the two contractors who have been successful in using the stewardship contract authority and one contractor, who through a demonstration project, helped pave the way for successful stewardship contracting in this area.

Contractor Lomakatsi (Ashland, Oregon) is a "non-profit organization, which develops and implements pro-active community based ecological restoration projects throughout the Klamath–Siskiyou bioregion of southwestern Oregon and northwestern California. Since 1995, our projects have assisted in the regeneration, rehabilitation, and restoration of ecologically degraded ecosystems throughout the region, with a strong emphasis on the development of Community Based Forestry and Watershed Stewardship Programs that cross land ownership boundaries."

Lomakatsi was the primary contractor for the Penny Stewardship project. On this project, they combined restoration forestry practices with low-impact tree harvesting systems.

Lomakatsi managers Justin Cullumbine (left) and Marko Bey (right)

Marko Bey, Director of Lomakatsi Operations, said that this was their "first Federal land project, but certainly not our first Federal funding for fuels reduction projects in the region. Since 2001, we have been awarded 11 National Fire Plan grants through BLM to perform fuels reduction on private land adjacent to federal land, mill and market the byproducts harvested, and train the workforce in restoration forestry."

Justin Cullumbine, Lomakatsi Program Coordinator, said that they have a formal training program with a curriculum that includes on-the-ground experience. "Our biggest hurdles are finances, producing products that actually bring in a profit, and finding niche markets. Our greatest success is in keeping our workers busy and re-training other crews in our ecological approach."

Lomakatsi has created a "green collar workforce" of skilled ecosystem practitioners still guided by experts in many fields, including Traditional Ecological Knowledge. Lomakatsi has applied their "*Ecological Principles for Fuels Reduction and Restoration*" on thousands of acres of private, municipal and federal lands, across the region, and convened more than 60 trainings for 300 people.

"The Penny Stewardship project was a bridge builder within the community. It also helped pave the way for future stewardship projects," Justin added. "We continue to be called upon by that community as the model of practices that they prefer and the practitioners they trust."

Before performing the actual work on the Penny Stewardship project, Lomakatsi set up a team of economic consultants, community residents, and members of other local groups who were very interested in seeing this project handled with an ecological restoration focus. This group worked together to design the best forest restoration treatments for the Penny Stewardship project.

The Penny project included a mixture of ponderosa and sugar pines, white and black oaks, and Pacific madrone. Lomakatsi applied a variety of restoration methods, from thinning small trees, retaining the largest and healthiest trees to burning smaller fuels, and reseeding burn piles with native grasses.

Lomakatsi's goals were to reduce wildfire intensity, modify the configuration of plants and fuels, reduce fuel loads along roads and landscape areas, enhance wildlife habitat, control invasive species, and provide appropriate erosion control.

Also, Marko said that because Lomakatsi had worked primarily on private lands before this project, they were eager to demonstrate on public land their ecological restoration work as a sustainable model for fuels reduction and byproduct utilization.

Lomakatsi hosted a series of educational workshops, one of which included 150 area residents, environmental organization members, and BLM personnel. Many people remained engaged, regularly touring the project at each stage of the process.

"We worked closely with BLM during the Penny Stewardship project and have developed a great partnership with BLM. We are focused on contributing to the long-term economic sustainability by developing a workforce to work on these projects," Marko said.

Over time, Lomakatsi has become a dedicated mentor in providing technical assistance and training to small-scale forestry-related businesses, contractors, and communities.

Their forest restoration projects have provided merchantable logs and alternative wood products to the local forest economy, jobs to local residents, and a level of community involvement in forestry operations never before experienced in southwestern Oregon.

Chris Rusch, BLM Tiller Ranger District botanist and silviculturist, says about Lomakatsi, "They are professional, responsive, and knowledgeable in the area of stewardship contracting."

Contractor Don Hamann (Butte Falls, Oregon) is one of the most passionate and kind people you will ever meet. He is not driven by money or prestige. He truly cares and is motivated about doing what's right for the land. He is a forestry contractor who sometimes enlists the assistance of several subcontractors on his projects.

Hamann said he became tired of just production logging for the industry people and wanted to focus on forest improvement. "I got involved with stewardship contracting through networking with BLM people. When stewardship contracting came along, it opened the door for me. It is definitely a learning process for both BLM and the contractor, but BLM does a great job of helping me through the process. "

Don Hamann (left), Butte Falls, Oregon

George McKinley (left) and Blair Moody (BLM, right)

Regarding completing the necessary paperwork for stewardship contracting, he says "It is quite a procedure to put it all together. It took a couple of weeks of work and I had a lot of help. Stewardship contracting is not for everybody—lots of logistics, planning, and marketing. We need stable markets and supply to make contracting work."

Hamann feels that stewardship contracting ties in well with economic development and training people for the future, which is a must for improving the land for the next generation. He is extremely motivated and rewarded by looking back on what they have accomplished over the past 25 years.

"One of the things I like best about stewardship contracting is coordinating the people and developing a team. It's satisfying to see when the guys finally get a hold of it and then get it. They are excited about what they do. They start to develop the proper thinking about taking care of our natural resources," says Hamann.

Hamann usually has a crew of six. "When we get more work, we hire more." He uses mostly standard logging equipment.

Jack LeRoy, one of Hamann's subcontractors, recently purchased a purpose-built machine designed to remove

small-diameter material economically. It has low ground pressure—4.5 pounds per square inch. Leroy says that "The technique you use for each application is very important. Every acre has a difference application, different slope, and different type of timber. It is very difficult to find one machine that fits all."

"It takes many within the community such as BLM, subcontractors, the working crew, and even our end market folks working together to accomplish the task. We support each other. We share workers, trucks, equipment, etc.," says Hamann.

Hamann notes that "The community is now starting to see the philosophy behind stewardship contracting and that it works. I feel like we are passing the torch on to the next generation."

Contractor George McKinley (Ashland, Oregon), owner of Mountain Millworks, worked closely with BLM long before there were stewardship contracts. It was McKinley who set the stage for stewardship contracting in this area.

McKinley moved to Oregon in 1992. He grew up in the Midwest, where his family had a Christmas tree business. As a young student, he left the Midwest to attend college in Oregon, where he has lived ever since.

McKinley says "As a result of owning land, I got engaged with forestry; I eventually bought some land and became very concerned about the management of forest lands. I began to see the importance of public lands and wanted to become more involved in better management of public land, probably from an environmental perspective. I felt that doing nothing was one of the worst things we could do as far as taking care of public lands."

To get more involved, McKinley headed up the Boaz Forest Health and Small-Diameter Utilization Project. This demonstration project was a collaboration between the Jefferson Sustainable Development Initiative and the Medford District Bureau of Land Management. The project was implemented during the field seasons of 2004–2006.

The goal of this project was to enhance forest health and provide regional employment through a collaborative project to remove and process small-diameter material.

Project objectives included assessing technical and economic feasibility, monitoring forest health and fire hazard reduction, determining market opportunities for small-diameter material, expanding the capacity of the rural work force, improving community/agency relations, and informing policy discussions at various levels.

During this project, McKinley took hundreds of people interested in this project out to tour the site, explaining the environmental aspect, stand characteristics, the type of

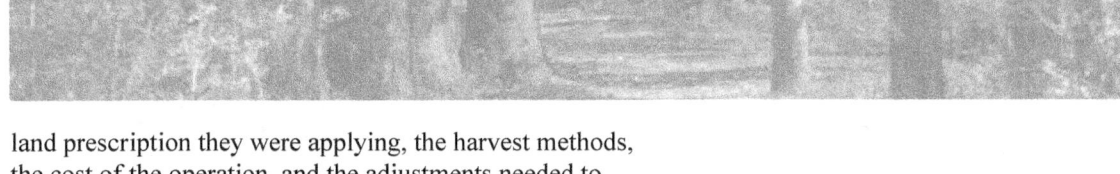

land prescription they were applying, the harvest methods, the cost of the operation, and the adjustments needed to improve revenue. Eventually he wrote a report discussing the entire project, which included his results and recommendations.

His primary finding was "restoration and management focused upon the utilization of smaller, underutilized material is more cost effective and achieves broader goals than fuel treatments focused on piling and burning alone."

McKinley said that this project "Changed his thinking on the opportunities in the forest."

According to Blair Moody, BLM District Lead: Biomass, Small Diameter, Stewardship Contracting, Medford District Office, "As a result of this project, George basically established the baseline for stewardship contracts in this area."

McKinley expresses deep gratitude to BLM, especially to Blair Moody, for his leadership and guidance and the expertise of folks at the Watershed Research and Training Center, in Hayfork, California.

"Looking back," McKinley says, "I realize the most important ingredients in the implementation of an on-the-ground collaborative endeavor are partners that practice trust, flexibility, and patience. Strong partners and skilled workers are essential."